SPRING SUN, LOTUS FLOWER

Quotes from the
Teachings of Venerable Master
Hsuan Hua

DRBA/BTTS/DRBU

Published and translated by:

Buddhist Text Translation Society
1777 Murchison Drive, Burlingame, CA 94010-4504

© 2004 Buddhist Text Translation Society
        Dharma Realm Buddhist University
        Dharma Realm Buddhist Association

First edition 2004

ISBN 0-88139-939-6

Printed in Malaysia

Addresses of the Dharma Realm Buddhist Association
branches are listed at the back of this book.

        Library of Congress Cataloging-in-Publication Data

Hsuan Hua, 1908-
    Spring sun, lotus flower: quotes from the teachings of
Venerable Master Hsuan Hua.
        p. cm.
    ISBN 0-88139-939-6 (alk. paper)
    1.   Buddhism—Social aspects. 2. Conduct of life. I.
Title: Quotes from the teachings of Venerable Master Hsuan
Hua. II. Title.

  BQ4570.S6H75 2004
  294.3'4—dc22   CIP 2003024525

SPRING
SUN,
LOTUS
FLOWER

Preface

by Martin Verhoeven

Like the China of Great Master Hsuan-tsang's time, America in the late 20th century is awash with a staggering variety of Buddhisms. Just as wave after wave of divergent Indian Buddhist schools and sects inundated China from the end of the Han up through the Tang, so have we witnessed in the West an equally rich and perplexing infusion of schools and teachings—all purporting to be genuine, orthodox, the "real teaching." Great Master Hsuan-tsang (c. 586-664) sought to resolve the confusion of so many conflicting opinions by pilgrimaging to India to seek out the genuine Dharma for himself at its source, and to bring back the sacred scriptures to his homeland.

A great scholar and translator and one of the few Chinese to have mastered Sanskrit, Great Master Hsuan-tsang's stupendous journey marked a high point in the transmission of Buddhism from one culture to another. Americans now, like the Chinese of the Sui and Tang, long for the same clarity and voice of authority. Ironically, the Great Master Hsuan-tsang may have had an easier time in his quest than contemporary seekers.

For even when the texts became readily available to Americans (available in a quantity and quality perhaps unequaled in history), the "reading" of those texts proved far more difficult and daunting than we imagined. As the Great Master Hsuan-tsang discovered, and as we Americans are belatedly discovering, Buddhism—the real and vital Buddhism—is penetrated not simply through reading texts (however carefully) and learned exegeses, but through a far more subtle and interior process called "self-cultivation."

Another irony: Where Great Master Hsuan-tsang had to risk life and limb traversing god-forsaken deserts and freezing mountains to find the teachings of enlightenment and wise mentors, we in America find both teachings and teachers arriving practically on our doorsteps. Since the 1890s and especially since World War II, Buddhism and Buddhist masters have clearly set the Dharma on a new course: from East to West, from Asia to America. This fragile transfer of ancient wisdom to the New World, as with all previous migrations of the Dharma to new lands, however, depends for its success on transplanting not simply the scriptures, but transmitting the "living tradition." Only on the strength and inspiration of living examples of Buddhism does the Dharma take root in fresh soil and grow in new hearts. Such an exemplar was Venerable Master Hsuan Hua. And such was the scope of his vow: to bring the Dharma to America.

It was this living example of a great soul "manifesting a body to speak the Dharma," that made Buddhism come alive for me and I am sure for many others who met the Master. And it is in those meetings, those person-to-person encounters, that the Master's spirit continues to live. What he instilled by his example and tireless giving to each individual he met, insures in some ineffable way that the Dharma will continue to live—to live not just in translations, but in the boundless living beings who had the privilege and opportunity to be kindled and transformed by his light.

VENERABLE MASTER
HSUAN HUA

The Venerable Master Hsuan Hua was also known as An Tse and To Lun. The name Hsuan Hua was bestowed upon him after he received the transmission of the Wei Yang Lineage of the Chan School from Venerable Elder Hsu Yun. He left the home life at the age of nineteen. After the death of his mother, he lived in a tiny thatched hut by her grave-side for three years, as an act of filial respect. During that time, he practiced meditation and studied the Buddha's teachings. Among his many practices were eating only once a day at midday and never lying down to sleep.

In 1948 the Master arrived in Hong Kong, where he founded the Buddhist Lecture Hall and other monasteries. In 1962 he brought the Proper Dharma to America and the West, where he lectured extensively on the major works of the Mahayana Buddhist canon and established the Dharma Realm Buddhist Association, as well as the City of Ten Thousand Buddhas, the International Translation Institute, various other monastic facilities, Dharma Realm Buddhist University, Developing Virtue Secondary School, Instilling Goodness Elementary School, the vocational Sangha and Laity Training Programs, and other education centers.

The Master passed into stillness on June 7, 1995, in Los Angeles, California, USA, causing many people throughout the world to mourn the sudden setting of the sun of wisdom. Although his life has passed on, his lofty example will always be remembered. Throughout his life he worked selflessly and vigorously to benefit the people of the world and all living beings. His wisdom and compassion inspired many to correct their faults and lead wholesome lives.

Here we include the Records of the Mendicant of Chang Bai written by the Venerable Master to serve as a model for all of us to emulate.

The Mendicant of Chang Bai was simple and honest in nature.
He was always quick to help people and benefit others.
Forgetting himself for the sake of the Dharma, he was willing to sacrifice his life.
Bestowing medicines according to peoples illnesses, he offered his own marrow and skin.
His vow was to unite in substance with millions of beings.
His practice exhausted empty space as he gathered in the myriad potentials,
Without regard for past, future, or present;

Part One

If we want to learn to have genuine wisdom, we must first cut off desire. How do we cut off desire? By not fighting, not being greedy, not seeking, not being selfish, not pursuing personal advantage, and not lying. These six great principles are the Dharma jewels for cutting off desire and obtaining genuine wisdom.

What does upholding the precepts mean? It means not fighting, not being greedy, not seeking, not being selfish, not pursuing personal advantage, and not telling lies.

When a proper person practices deviant dharma, even the deviant dharma becomes proper. When a deviant person practices proper dharma, even the proper dharma becomes deviant.

Why can't people dwell in harmony in the world? They fight with and rob each other and don't yield to each other. Therefore wars break out, leading to the tragic situation of countries being destroyed and families going to ruin.

Buddhist disciples should endure starvation, endure cold, endure thirst, and endure hunger. Everything we disciples do should accord with the Buddhadharma. We should not be greedy to eat good food, wear good clothes, or live in fine places. We should not be greedy for enjoyment. Enduring suffering puts an end to suffering, but enjoying blessings uses up blessings.

People who are greedy are never happy. If they are not greedy, they will be happy. Therefore, we should put an end to greed.

In cultivation, we should apply effort naturally. We should not be greedy and ask whether there is any efficacy or whether there will be good results. We should not think about anything, but just keep applying effort and changing our faults everyday.

Basically, there is only one precept—not being selfish. If people are selfish, they will violate the precepts. If they are not selfish, they will not violate the precepts.

In cultivating, we have to turn things around. What does that mean? It means we give the good things to others, and keep the bad things for ourselves. We give up the small self in order to realize the great self.

If you can benefit people and make them happy, then no matter where you go, everyone will be influenced by your example.

If we lie, then no matter what mantra we recite, it will not be efficacious. Nor will any Sutra we recite have efficacy. If we want to be able to recite mantras or recite Sutra and obtain a response or have some accomplishment, then we cannot lie. We must be honest and speak true and actual words, not false or frivolous words.

The ancient sages always blamed themselves. Modern people, however, look for faults in others instead of acknowledging their own faults.

Patience means: "If people scold me, I can bear it. If they hit me, I can take it. No matter how badly they treat me, I can endure it."

There are no doors to the hells; you yourself make the doors.

Be gentle and agreeable. Avoid a hot temper. Do not be frightened under any circumstances.

With this body of yours, you ought to do some work and make a contribution to the world.

Practice of the way requires perseverance, sincerity, and determination.

If we want to make daily progress, we must become stricter with ourselves each day. We must become more collected and focused by not indulging in discursive thoughts.

If we avoid praising, criticizing, and bearing grudges against others, our mind will be peaceful and free from greed, anger, and delusion.

If we have no obstacles in our own minds, then outer obstacles will not hinder us or cause us worry.

What I stress is genuine merit and real practice, not false publicity.

We should always maintain an attitude of deep respect and make obeisance to the great Bodhisattvas of the ten directions. For every bit of respect we have, we will gain a bit of response. If we are one hundred percent respectful, we will gain the benefit of a total response.

All the various kinds of precepts are aimed at helping people follow the rules. People who follow the rules can help maintain order in society and resolve the problems faced by humankind. Thus, the moral precepts are the basis for world peace.

The Buddha's wisdom and radiance are like the sun, because they shine upon the entire earth, lighting up even the remotest dark corners.

Always be honest and open in your speech and actions.
Do not be sneaky or evasive with anyone. A straight mind is a Bodhimanda.

Studying Buddhism is worth more than any amount of money you might amass. In terms of your Dharma body and wisdom life, the Dharma is far more important than money. Don't take worldly wealth so seriously.

The Dharma is spoken, but the way has to be practiced. In order to derive benefit, we have to actually practice according to the Dharma.

Because of desires for illusory fame and profit, our minds are never at ease. This is where we differ from the Buddhas.

The reason we haven't obtained a response in our practice of Buddhism is that we have too many doubts.

"The spirits and immortals of old had no special tricks; they were simply happy as could be, and they never worried." This should be the motto of all cultivators.

We should know that nothing in the world comes easily; how can we expect a reward when we haven't put in the work?

If we did not fight, were not greedy, did not seek anything, were not selfish, and did not want to benefit ourselves, we would have no anger.

We should not say things that cause people to entertain thoughts of lust. We should not tell improper jokes, use suggestive language or casually discuss such topics.

All afflictions are based on selfishness. That is why we have so much anger and so many troubles.

What ordinary people are most attached to is the emotional love between men
and women.

If you don't develop Dharma-selecting vision—the genuine wisdom to distinguish between the Dharma and what is not the Dharma—you will have studied the Dharma in vain.

If you want to regain your treasury of the Tathagata, you first have to protect your essence, energy, and spirit. Those are your treasures.

If you want to determine whether a person is genuine or phony, whether he is Bodhisattva or a demon, you can look for the following things: First, see whether he has any desire for sex; and second, see whether he is greedy for money.

It is not easy to eliminate our faults, but, if we can eradicate our faults, we will have samadhi power.

Those who see our faults are our teachers. We should be thankful to them instead of resentful.

Those who truly understand cultivation do the work right within their daily activities. Every act constitutes cultivation.

We should nurture our energy
and not expend it in fits of temper.

Why do people lie? They are
afraid of losing personal
advantages; they don't want to take
loss.

After doing something, forget it and go on to the next matter. Nothing should be taken as ultimately real. As the Vajra Sutra says: "All conditioned phenomena are like dreams, illusions, bubbles, and shadows, like dew drops or flashes of lightning. One should contemplate them thus."

If our intellect does not discriminate between hot and cold, then they do not exist. When hot and cold do not exist, who could feel them? The same principle is true of all conditioned things. If we refrain from making unnecessary distinctions, our original peace of mind remains undisturbed.

With genuine wisdom you won't be upside-down. Why do people often make mistakes? It is because they haven't developed their true wisdom. Without wisdom, thoughts, words, and deeds fail to accord with the Dharma.

One should dwell in a small and humble home, eat light meals, have a good disposition, and put an end to one's karma.

How can one become a Buddha? Becoming a Buddha involves not fighting, not being greedy, not seeking, not being selfish, not pursuing personal advantage, and not lying. You say, "Is it that simple?" Yes, it's that simple!

Neither loving nor hating anything is the Middle Way. We speak of cultivating the Way, but what is this Way that we cultivate? It is the Middle Way—treating everyone with equanimity, kindness and compassion.

In our daily cultivation, we should maintain an attitude of calm equanimity, meaning we should be placid and serene at all times, without any ripples or waves in our natures. That's what's meant by "afflictions are bodhi." And "birth and death are nirvana."

"Firewood gathered in a thousand days can be completely burned up by a single match."

The "single match" points to our tempers. You may accumulate a thousand days worth of merit and virtue, but if you lose your temper once, you burn up all that merit and virtue.

Why is it that cultivators of the Way should not eat meat? It's because eating meat increases people's sexual desire. Cultivators do not want to arouse sexual desire, and so they should consume food and drink which do not stimulate desire.

The precepts are alive. When you know that something accords with the Buddhadharma, then it is a precept. Things that go against the Dharma are not precepts.

The Buddha is identical to space. There is a saying, "If people want to understand the state of a Buddha, they should make their minds as pure as space." Space has no marks and is boundless.

A Buddha's substance resembles space.

The essential quality of the Way is concentration; that of a general is his strategic skill, not his courage; that of an army is its quality, not its size.

We may think we are doing good deeds, but they are not necessarily good deeds.

That's because the "seeds" or causes may not be pure.

When a defiled thought arises,
you are in the saha world.

Why are we subject to birth and
death? It is due to our confused
thoughts.

If you do not know how to use the Buddhadharma, it is like having a bright pearl sewn in your clothing and not knowing about it. Once you discover the bright pearl, you can use it. The bright pearl can give you all kinds of treasures. You can use it forever, and it will never wear out.

People's daily lives consist of such matters as eating and sleeping. But you have to know how to do them; otherwise there will be problems. Thus, with food and drink, you should neither go too hungry, nor stuff yourself. Going to either extreme, indicates that you lack sufficient patience.

Don't fail to do any work, but also don't work too hard. Do as much work as you have the energy to do. We should do some things for the sake of others in the world. We should make our contribution.

The regulation of our intake of food, our sleep, our bodies, and our breath is done by our minds. How should one's mind be regulated? It should not be sunk into a torpor, nor should it be too high-strung and excited. One should keep it calm and quiet.

How do we become Buddhas? We must enlighten ourselves, enlighten others, and perfect enlightenment and practice. At that point, we will be Buddhas.

What is confusion? It is to take suffering as happiness and right as wrong; to mix up black and white; to fail to distinguish between true and false; and to regard what is transitory as external.

To see things as they are is to understand; to let go of them is to be liberated; to be liberated is to be one's own master.

What is the "real me"? It is the inherent nature and the attainment of Buddhahood. Only when one attains Buddhahood, can one find the "real me." Before that, everything is false.

The hope of becoming enlightened; the hope of becoming a Buddha—even these are false thoughts. Everyone should remember this point: we should be concerned only with cultivation and not cling to hopes.

Why don't we have any response in the way? It's because our wild minds never rest.

I consider all religions to be one family, and so I call Buddhism the teaching of living beings.

If we do ghostly things, we are
ghosts.
If we act like human beings, we
are human beings.
If we do the deeds of Buddhas,
we become Buddhas.

We should recognize that advances in science and in material benefits are not necessarily good for humanity in the long run. They are incomplete, imperfect benefits. Wisdom, on the other hand, is the most comprehensive benefit for the whole world. Thinking and attitudes born of morality and virtue are thoroughly good for us all.

The Buddha's four measureless attitudes of kindness, compassion, joy, and even-mindedness are totally advantageous to all creatures. When we base ourselves in thoughts such as these, then we can go ahead and put technology to work for us.

Don't get scared when you hear me call television, radios, and computers "man-eating goblins." No need to be afraid. My hope is that you will clearly recognize these things for what they are. Once you recognize them, those electric gadgets lose their power to confuse you.

But if you're confused by them, then they can gobble you down.

Regardless of your method of practice, as long as you have patience, you will make headway. If you lack patience, then you won't be successful with any method of practice.

Why is it that we cannot recognize our original face? It's because we haven't demolished our mark of self and selfishness.

Cultivators should cultivate the Way in order to end birth and death and cross over living beings. They should not be cultivating with the hope of obtaining a response.

$\mathcal{L}$et us bring forth our true mind in studying the Buddhadharma. Our every move and action, our every word and deed needs to be true.

Those who truly practice Chan meditation, truly chant the Buddha's name as well. Those who can really recite the Buddha's name are, in fact, investigating Chan meditation. Chan practice and Buddha recitation both help us stop our idle thoughts and sweep away our personal desires and random thoughts, so that our original face can appear.

The Buddha concentrated only on transcendental dharmas, and so he was unstained by worldly dharmas. Like empty space, he was as a clean breath of fresh air.

In walking, standing, sitting, and lying down, we should always be attentive. We should be aware of everything we say and do.

We should look after ourselves. Don't be like a washing machine that washes other people's clothes, but in the process gets dirty itself.

For each bit of sincerity we bring forth, we will receive a bit of response. If we are ten parts sincere, we will have a ten parts of response. If we are a hundred percent sincere, we will have a hundred percent response. The supreme, profound, wondrous Dharma is difficult for anyone to encounter in life.

Since we have encountered it now, we must do our best to put it into practice.

PART TWO

I am as a small ant, content to crawl beneath the feet of all living beings.

I am as a road, existing so all living beings can walk upon me and travel from the stage of ordinary beings to the stage of Buddhas.

We want to do what is difficult
to do. We want to be as candles
that can withstand the wind,
and be as pure gold that can
withstand smelting in a blazing
furnace.

Everything is a test, to see what you will do.
If you do not recognize what is before you, you will have to start anew.

A true mind and true intent bring truth within truth. True practice and true cultivation take the truth beyond truth.

True behavior and true conduct add truth to truth.

In everything and every way, be true, true, true.

The affairs of the world are impermanent; don't be attached to them. In dreamlike samadhi, one is free and at ease. Roaming playfully with spiritual powers, One accords with changes and transformations. In stillness, contemplate all things; their glory fades by itself.

If you cannot give up death,
You cannot exchange it for life.
If you cannot give up what is false,
You will not accomplish what is
true.

The door through which I was born is also the threshold of my death. How many of us are astute; how many enlightened?
In the middle of the night, the hero is absorbed in self-reflection; One must stop the turning wheel of birth and death by oneself.

When every thought is sincere,
every thought penetrates; In
silence, responses are quietly
received.

When you reach the end of the
mountains and rivers,
You are free to roam throughout
the Dharma Realm.

Dhyana Paramita is a Sanskrit term, Meaning still reflection and subtle investigation.

The mountains are lofty and the waters are deep, But there is nothing to fear; One begins to know that beyond this world is another world.

The wondrous principles of the Buddhadharma are basically ineffable.

After awakening, a single word is too much.

But because living beings have deep confusion, Words are spoken as skillful expedients.

Purge the fire in your liver, and avoid all disease; Such a fine cure-all medicine—set on the shelf and forgotten! Suo po he!

In cultivating the Way, one must have a sincere mind.

If you are false, you may cheat yourself, But it's hard to cheat the spirits. Be cautious when you are alone and always maintain proper thoughts.

Don't do anything that goes against your conscience
in a dark room.

A greedy mind is like a bottomless pit. Because it is hard to fill, anger arises. A profusion of the five desires leads to upside-down thinking.
Without our realizing it, the Dharma vessel disintegrates.

Truly recognize your own faults.
Don't discuss the faults of others.
Others' faults are just your own.
To be one with everyone is called
Great Compassion.

You don't have to believe in me
or believe in the Buddha.
Believe in your own inherent
wisdom.
Discover the Prajna in your own
nature, Then you'll attain Dharma-
selecting vision.

Depressed and melancholy, you
roam through the hells.
Happy and smiling, you enjoy
eternal youth.
Weeping and woe make a small
dark room in the hells.

The great mantra of great compassion penetrates heaven and earth.

One hundred recitations for one thousand days cause ten kings to rejoice.

Its great compassion and kindness cure all diseases, And so an announcement is projected high upon the offense screen.

To always be vigorous is to be in samadhi.

To accord with conditions without changing one's principles is Vajra samadhi.

Vajra samadhi has no fixed form; It is simply the indestructible resolve for Bodhi.

Every person's body is a prison cell. It's just that we don't realize it.

Cultivation requires a calm, peaceful mind devoid of affliction and conceit.

Always seeking within yourself means truly recognizing your own faults and never discussing the faults of others.

Two requisites of cultivation are compassion and humility.

We must be kind and compassionate to everyone.

We must also be humble, not arrogant and not attached to the Four Marks (self, others, being, and life span).

We must destroy all attachments before we can practice the Bodhisattva path.

As we study the Buddhadharma, every day we should become more and more intelligent, not more and more stupid. If you can take being scolded by others, then you have real skill in patience. Don't scold others or lose your temper at them.

When you thoroughly understand all matters and principles, it is especially important to keep a low profile.

Bowing to the Buddhas is extremely important. Unless there are exceptional circumstances, everyone should be in attendance for bowing to the Buddhas. Bowing is an excellent activity; it is good exercise that makes you physically and mentally healthy and improves your circulation. If you do such exercise, you will be cured of all illness.

What is wisdom? It is a manifestation of selflessness. What is idle thinking? It is an indication of selfishness. Once selfishness takes hold, idle thoughts arise.

Dharma, the teaching of the Buddha, permeates and penetrates everywhere. There are no fixed Dharmas. Dharmas are constant in the way that the water of a river flows smoothly on and is not attached in any place. If you say that a Dharma is fixed, then it immediately becomes a dead Dharma. The Vajra Sutra says, "one should produce the thought that dwells nowhere." This is what meant by "no fixed Dharma."

People in the Dharma-Ending Age tend to make a common mistake; they shoot for the moon and stumble over their own feet. They trade their eyes for ears, take hearsay for fact and go pursue it.

In cultivation, making vows is very important. Patience is also of the utmost importance. Anyone who can be patient will surely succeed in accomplishing the Way. Patience is the ability to endure adversity as if it were as pleasant as eating honey, without getting the least bit upset or angry. That's what's required to accomplish the practice of patience and perfect one's work in the Way.

The proper Dharma consists of: not fighting, not being greedy, not seeking, not being selfish, not wanting personal advantages, and not telling lies. These are known as the six great guidelines. No matter what Dharma it is, you may use the six guidelines as a yardstick to measure, judge, and assess it. If it accords with the six rules, it can be called a proper Dharma. If it goes against them, it is a deviant Dharma.

Humankind has invented many things that are of great benefit. However, humankind has also invented hydrogen and atomic bombs. With these have come various bizarre diseases that are difficult to cure. Modern conveniences bring both benefit and disaster. Therefore, in the midst of good, there is bad; in the midst of bad, there is good.

Don't worry about things that are already past. While doing things, use your wisdom to ensure that they are done well. When they are completed, do not continue to think about them. Quiet your mind. It is best to view life as a play, and not think of it as being too real; then fewer worries and problems will bother you. You will be able to come and go with freedom and independence.

Whatever we do in cultivation of the Way, we shouldn't get angry. Whether people are good to us or not, we should maintain thoughts of loving kindness, compassion, and protection for them. We shouldn't feel hatred toward anyone, or be upset by him or her. It won't be a problem if we perfect our cultivation. But if we remain in the Triple Realm, we will have to undergo retribution for our hatred.

You will reap the fruit of whatever cause you plant now. Why do we suffer so much now? It's because in the distant past we didn't cultivate enough good roots. That's why we have so many misfortunes and disappointments now. We try hard to be good to people but they misunderstand us or deliberately test us. When that kind of thing happens, return the light and look within.

Reputation, profit, wealth, beauty, fame, food, and sleep are things that worldly people like. For people who like to eat good food, one kind is not enough. They demand a variety of dishes. And the better the food, the more their appetite grows.

Thus, food is a worldly dharma, as is clothing. There are others who enjoy wearing fine clothes. When one is defiled by worldly dharmas, one cannot achieve transcendental dharma.

When worldly dharmas prevail, transcendental dharma seems insignificant.

If what is good and what is not good are seen as fundamentally without difference, then we will not have problems. If we discriminate good as good, and not good as not good, then we will be turned by external states of mind.

If we pursue external states, then the more we run, the further we stray from our original home. If we are not moved, we remain in our original home. We should view our bodies as if they were heaven and earth. Between them, heaven and earth include the myriad things, and yet are not separate from them. If we understand this principle, nothing in the world can torment or worry us.

Here's how the world turns: Good taken to the ultimate point turns bad. Evil, once it reaches an extreme, turns good. A person who is poverty-stricken can suddenly strike it rich, while rich people can lose every penny overnight. At birth, we are in the cycle of coming into being and ceasing to be that rolls on in this world.

It is a natural process of progression, cyclical change and transformation. If we recognize that process, then getting rich won't especially appeal to us any longer. And if we should lose our wealth, then we will see things according to the proverb: "The superior person, even in poverty, maintains his integrity. The petty person stops at nothing to strike it rich."

The Great Bodhi Way is straight
as can be. Don't let yourself get
sidetracked or try to find a
shortcut. If you seek the Dharma
with a true heart, There's sure to
be a response.
If you are insincere and negligent,
you're just wasting time.

Advance vigorously, be patient, and don't retreat!

Practice giving, uphold the precepts, and cultivate wisdom.

One day you will complete the journey to the other shore.

And join the Buddhas of the ten directions at the lotus pool.

If you ask me why I'm laughing;
Let me first ask you why you're
crying.
Crying and laughing are not the
middle way.
Why should we be attached to the
two sides!"

In one gulp, he swallows the tears of sorrow and resentment. His two eyes see through those who are involved in fame and gain.

No one recognizes this Bodhisattva.

They all miss him at arm's length.

They are still wandering about wasting time.

Question: Where do wars come from?

Venerable Master: From the violent energy in our minds. Our minds don't have harmonious energy; that is why we have wars.

Question: Why are there so many earthquakes nowadays?

Venerable Master: Because people have great tempers.

Question: It has been said, "On the astronomical scale, man is insignificant." Yet man is also the "astronomer."

Who, then, is insignificant?

Venerable Master: People are not small and the universe is not big. If there were no people, then there would be no universe. If it were not for people, then there would be no ghosts and no Buddhas either, because it is only people who recognize them. Without people, what possible function could the Buddha perform? It is all made by us, and we are part of it.

Question: There is a great deal of ignorance and misunderstanding among westerners with regard to Buddhism. This is strange considering the great advancements made in communications. Of course, it seems that truth and falseness are communicated with equal speed.

Venerable Master: Good and bad as well as true and false exist only because people recognize them as such. Originally there is no true and false; people establish them. So what you think of as true is true, and what you think of as false is false.

The *Avatamsaka Sutra* says, "Everything is made from the mind alone." Science, technology, and philosophy, all progress. Where do they come from? They come from the mind.

Question: There are many sects in Buddhism. What about that?

Venerable Master: All religions, as well as everything else, manifest in response to the karmic conditions of living beings. The Buddhadharma is no different from any other religion.

The more principle you understand, the less is it necessary to discuss little points. The more expansive the principle you speak, the closer you approach truth.

Originally all religions were established to regulate conduct, so that people would not do any bad, but instead offer up all good. But as soon as people discriminate, sectarianism appears, and people are soon offering up all bad. Where sectarianism develops, there is often a great deal of quarreling.

Question: Isn't it true that Buddhism is higher than all other religions?

Venerable Master: There is no high or low with respect to religions. Religions are simply medicines to cure human ills. After having taken enough medicine to completely cure the illness, why continue to take medicine? The Buddhadharma explains that everything is the result of the karmic causes and conditions of living beings. It is not the case that I or anyone else tells you to do what you do. Nothing you do is imposed from without. All that manifests is reward or retribution for the karmic actions of human beings.

Question: Do you believe that we are capable of determining and controlling the course of our individual destines?

Venerable Master: It is not fixed. What happens to us depends on what we do, and what we want to do. You can become president and so can I.

It only requires that we expend the necessary effort and do what is required to reach our desired goal.

In the Buddhadharma, equality is found even in the realm of the Buddhas. All Buddhas are equal. It is not that some Buddhas are bigger than others, some taller and some shorter, some better and some worse, some lighter and some darker. All Buddhas are in accord and they have no mutual obstruction.

ᴅHARMA REALM BUᴅᴅHISᴛ ASSOCIAᴛIOᴎ

The Dharma Realm Buddhist Association (DRBA) was founded by the Venerable Master Hsuan Hua in the United States of America in 1959 to bring the genuine teachings of the Buddha to the entire world. Its goals are to propagate the Proper Dharma, to translate the Mahayana Buddhist scriptures into the world's languages and to promote ethical education. The members of the association guide themselves with six ideals established by the Venerable Master which are: no fighting, no greed, no seeking, no selfishness, no pursuing personal advantage, and no lying. They hold in mind the credo:

> Freezing, we do not scheme.
> Starving, we do not beg.
> Dying of poverty, we ask for nothing.
> According with conditions, we do not change.
> Not changing, we accord with conditions.

We adhere firmly to our three great principles.
We renounce our lives to do the Buddha's work.
We take responsibility in molding our own
    destinies.
We rectify our lives to fulfill our roles as
    members of the Sangha.
Encountering specific matters, we understand
    the principles.
Understanding the principles, we apply them in
    specific matters.
We carry on the single pulse of the patriarchs'
    mind-transmission.

During the following decades, international Buddhist communities such as Gold Mountain Monastery, the City of Ten Thousand Buddhas, the City of the Dharma Realm and various other branch facilities were founded. All these operate under the guidance of the Venerable Master and through the auspices of the Dharma Realm Buddhist Association. Following the Buddha's guidelines, the Sangha members in these monastic facilities maintain the practices of taking only one meal a day and of always wearing their precept sashes. Reciting the Buddha's name, studying the teachings, and practicing meditation, they dwell together in harmony and personally put into practice the Buddha's teachings.

Reflecting Master Hua's emphasis on translation and education, the Association also sponsors an International Translation Institute, Vocational Training Programs for the Sangha and the Laity, Dharma Realm Buddhist University, and Instilling Goodness Elementary & Developing Virtue Secondary Schools.

The Way-places of this Association are open to sincere individuals of all races, religions, and nationalities. Anyone willing to put forth his or her best effort in nurturing humaneness, merit and virtue in order to understand the mind and see the nature is welcome to join in the study and practice.

Dharma Realm Buddhist Association
The City of Ten Thousand Buddhas
4951 Bodhi Way, Ukiah, CA 95482 USA
Tel: (707) 462-0939 Fax: (707) 462-0949
Web site: http://**www.drba.org**

Institute for World Religions
(Berkeley Buddhist Monastery)
2304 McKinley Avenue,
Berkeley, CA 94703
Tel: (510) 848-3440

The International Translation Institute
1777 Murchison Drive,
Burlingame, CA 94010-4504
Tel: (650) 692-5912 Fax: (650) 692-5056

Gold Mountain Monastery
800 Sacramento Street,
San Francisco, CA 94108
Tel: (415) 421-6117 Fax: (415) 788-6001

Gold Sage Monastery
11455 Clayton Road,
San Jose, CA 95127
Tel: (408) 923-7243 Fax: (408) 923-1064

The City of the Dharma Realm
1029 West Capitol Avenue,
West Sacramento, CA 95691
Tel: (916) 374-8268

Gold Wheel Monastery
235 North Avenue 58,
Los Angeles, CA 90042
Tel: (323) 258-6668 Fax: (323) 258-3619

Gold Buddha Monastery
248 East 11th Avenue, Vancouver,
B.C. V5T 2C3 Canada
Tel: (604) 709-0248 Fax: (604) 684-3754

Gold Summit Monastery
233 1st Ave West,
Seattle, WA 98119
Tel: (206) 284-6690 Fax: (206) 284-6918

Long Beach Monastery
3361 East Ocean Boulevard,
Long Beach, CA 90803
Tel/Fax: (562) 438-8902

Blessings, Prosperity, and Longevity Monastery
4140 Long Beach Boulevard, Long Beach, CA 90807
Tel/Fax: (562) 595-4966

$6.95

Avatamsaka Vihara
9601 Seven Locks Road, Bethesda,
MD 20817-9997 USA
Tel/Fax: (301) 469-8300

Avatamsaka Monastery
1009 4th Avenue, S.W. Calgary,
AB T2P OK8 Canada
Tel/Fax: (403) 234-0644

Gold Dharma Monastery
3645 Florida Avenue Kenner, LA 70065 USA
Tel:(504) 466-1626

Dharma Realm Guanyin Sagely Monastery
161, Jalan Ampang, 50450 Kuala Lumpur, Malaysia
Tel: (03) 2164-8055 Fax: (03) 2163-7118

**Prajna Guanyin Sagely Monastery
(formerly Tze Yun Tung)**
Batu 5 1/2 Jalan Sungai Besi, Salak Selatan, 57100
Kuala Lumpur, Malaysia
Tel: (03) 7982-6560 Fax: (03) 7982-1272

**Dharma Realm Buddhist Books Distribution
Society**
11th Floor, 85 Chung-hsiao E. Road, Sec. 6,
Taipei, Taiwan R.O.C.
Tel: (02) 2786-3022 Fax: (02) 2786-2674